The Language of the Aids

written & illustrated by Christine Wolfe

Copyright ©2011 Christine Wolfe

www.the-language-of-the-aids.com
author@the-language-of-the-aids.com

Revised first edition

All rights reserved.
No part of this publication may be reproduced, stored in or introduced into a retrieval system, or transmitted in any form or by any means (electronic, mechanical, photocopying, recording, hand-written or otherwise), without the prior written permission of the author or her inheritors or any entity to whom the copyright may be transferred.

The horse on the cover was created by Bernt Wachtmeister (www.wachtmeister-art.de) and was found in an online collection of royalty-free clipart. The cover was laid out by the author.

ISBN-13: 978-0-9851963-0-1

self-published by the author
& printed by the Snowfall Press (Monument, Colorado, USA)

Dedication

to Ray Barry, who listens and sees with his brain.

Acknowledgments

My thanks to Ray Barry in his role as "guinea-pig",
to Olwen Wolfe, PhD, for her invaluable semiotics contributions
in designing the cover and the title page,
to Peter Blackwell for his observations
about the cover and the Introduction,
to Jan Blackwell & Molly Marks for their opinion about the title,
to Bonnie Smith & Smithbridge Stable in helping with its launch,
and to my many other friends who helped make this book possible.

Table of Contents

1	Introduction
3	Basic Principles
5	Gaits
9	The Ways in Which a Horse Can Move
15	The Natural Aids
25	A Note on Artificial Aids
27	School Figures
57	Drills
59	Conclusion
61	Appendices
	Bit Evasions
	Rider Removal
	Just Having Fun!

1   *The Language of the Aids*

Introduction

This book is more about the different ways you can communicate with the horse you are riding than it is about how to ride. The basics of human and equine psychology and physics are the same regardless of the riding style you choose.

The "aids" may be combined in ways dependent upon your knowledge and ability as well as your mount's talents and skills, and are traditionally referred to as "the language of the aids".

The natural "aids" include your voice, seat, legs and hands via the reins. It is the combination of these which allows you to ask your mount to perform specific tasks.

Within this book you will find the basic principles of my riding heritage, a description of gaits, a list of different movements you can ask a horse to perform as well as natural ways it can move, a description of the natural aids and a few artificial ones, descriptions and illustrations of school figures, and drills.

The Appendices list bit evasions and the different ways a horse can effectively remove its rider as well as a description of how a horse can have fun at your expense without necessarily causing a fall.

3   *The Language of the Aids*

Basic Principles

Ride by guile and with tact.
By "guile" is meant that you persuade your horse to believe that it wants to do what you want. This means that you cannot use force. Ask, do not tell.

By "tact" is meant that your movements follow its movements by moving your hands and seat with your mount. Not moving them will prevent it from going forwards freely. A freely moving horse is apt to be happy to have you ride it and will be more likely to be co-operative.

Using guile and tact will make it easier for your mount to use its neck as the balancing rod it is naturally designed for.

Ride using as little strength as possible.
Apply the aids with as little strength as possible. Use more only if the minimum does not work.

Ride with as litttle equipment as possible. A jointed snaffle is more than adequate for all but the most sophisticated work. All elementary work can be done with a jumping hackamore or a halter and rope. If you must ride with a bit, use the fattest, lightest one you can find.

If you cannot control your mount, look to yourself as the cause instead of using more severe equipment.

Keep your mount straight.
By "straight" is meant that the line or arc of your mount's spine exactly reflects the line or arc its feet travel.

Use any combination of aids to accomplish straightness. The aids which may work for you on one horse may not necessarily work on another. This is also true of aids another rider uses. This is why it is important not only to learn how to apply aids singly but also to experiment with them in order to find the best combinations for you.

The Language of the Aids

Control your mount's hindquarters by keeping it between your hand and your leg.
Use your seat and legs to drive your horse onto the bit to produce collection. A horse is collected when its hindquarters are engaged under itself, its frame appears shortened and it gives at the poll in a direct flexion.

In a proper direct flexion, the line of your horse's forehead and nose should be between five degrees outside the vertical and the vertical. If outside five degrees, the horse is not flexed enough at the poll while if within the vertical, the horse is said to be over-bent. Over-bending can impede breathing and may make a horse quite unhappy.

A collected horse feels as light as a feather because, in flexing at the poll and engaging its hindquarters, it has accepted your will.

Once collected, an educated horse can do virtually anything its rider asks.

The Language of the Aids

Gaits

The left side of a horse is said to be the near side because that is the side horses were mounted from by right-handed sword-wearing knights. The other side is called the off side. Using near and off lessens the confusion sometimes caused by using the word "right" because that word has several other meanings.

A horse almost invariably starts by moving a hind foot first. However, when spooking, it may move just one foot or all four at the same time.

The **Grazing Gait** is a four-beat diagonal one with three feet always on the ground. A stride starting from the near side consists of the near hind, off front, off hind and near front.

To my knowledge, noone else has ever noticed this pattern of foot-falls in a grazing horse and I doubt you will find it described anywhere else.

The instant a horse stops grazing and raises its head while moving, it shifts to some other gait.

The **Walk** is a four-beat lateral gait. A stride starting on the near side consists of the near hind, near front, off hind and off front. The horse usually has at least two feet in contact with the ground. Speeds range from close to zero to about four miles per hour, with the average being about two and half mph.

The flat-footed walk is a horse's natural travelling gait. Some horses perform the Spanish Walk, which is anything but natural and which requires considerable training and athleticism by both horse and rider. Gaited horses such as the Tennessee Walking Horse perform a genetic variation called the Running Walk; its foot-falls are so quick the horse appears to be running.

The Language of the Aids

The **Trot/Jog** is a two-beat diagonal hopping gait. A stride consists of alternating near and off diagonals. Only while at great speed is there is a moment of suspension between each stride.

The near diagonal is made up of the near front and off hind while the off one is made up of the off front and near hind. Speeds range from close to zero to about fifteen miles per hour. Most riding horses can go up to about eight mph while a racing trotter may be able to trot a mile in four minutes or less. The jog of a western-trained horse may be slower than its walk.

A horse trained to perform the Spanish Walk can also be taught the Spanish Trot. Gaited horses usually do not trot.

The **Pace/Amble** is a two-beat lateral rolling smooth gait which alternates pairs of feet. As with the trot, a slow-moving pacer always has two feet on the ground while a fast-moving one will have a moment of suspension between each beat. At racing speeds, a pacer may be slower than a trotter.

They swing their head and neck from side to side in order to keep their balance; in preventing this motion, a competent rider can make a pacer trot. Many gaited horses pace.

The **Canter/Lope** is a three-beat rolling gait. A stride starting on the near side consists of the near hind, near diagonal and off front, followed by a moment of suspension. A cantering horse is not necessarily faster than a trotting or pacing one.

Only a kangaroo at full hop or a human on a bicycle uses energy more efficiently than a cantering horse. However, only a physically fit horse should be allowed to canter for long periods of time. Movies notwithstanding, a horse normally travels at a walk.

All horses canter, whether gaited or not; the lope of a western-trained horse is actually a canter. Trained horses can perform a Spanish Canter.

The **Gallop** is actually a very fast canter with four beats instead of three. A stride starting from the near side consists of the near hind, off hind, near front and off front, followed by a moment of suspension.

Race horses can gallop up to 55 miles per hour. A jockey leans forwards to counter the g-force's tendency to whisk him/her off backwards. The speed of a gallopping riding horse is substantially slower; however, it is fast enough that not leaning forwards feels very uncomfortable.

The gallop is the gait used by frightened horses and is one best avoided unless used under controlled conditions in order to prevent horses from coming to potentially terminal grief.

Disunited canter and gallop

By "disunited" is meant an abnormal sequence of foot-falls in a stride.

The most common and the hardest to sense by a rider is the one in which a horse substitutes a lateral pair of feet for a diagonal one. In other words, a stride starting on the near side consists of the near hind, off pair and near front, followed by a moment of suspension.

More easily sensed is the sequence of near hind, off front, off hind and near front, or that of near hind, near fore, off hind and off front; either is followed by a moment of suspension.

A disunited gallop is also possible, with the same foot-fall variations.

The Language of the Aids

The **Reverse** is either a two-beat lateral gait or a two-beat diagonal one. All horses are capable of reversing but many are unwilling. Effective training may be best started in the stable using a voice command and praise, then transferring the voice command and the praise to your aids.

The Ways in Which a Horse Can Move

The controllable movements which may be performed by a horse are divided into three levels:

All non-gaited riding horses, regardless of the style used to ride them, should be able to walk, trot, canter, halt on command, turn left and right, and reverse.

While a bitted bridle is not necessary for work at this level, it is for all other levels since most require collection.

The exercises used to introduce horses to high-school work include direct and lateral flexions, leg-yielding, single Flying Changes, Half-passes, and single Turns on the Forehand and the Haunches at a walk.

High-school work includes:
- multiple Turns on the Forehand or the Haunches at a walk,
- the Pirouette (Turn on the Haunches at a canter),
- the Cadenced Trot (a slowed-down and rhythmic trot),
- the Passage (an even slower but just as rhythmic trot),
- the Piaffe (rhythmic slow trot on one spot),
- the Counter-canter (a collected canter on the wrong lead),
- multiple Flying Changes,
- all the Spanish gaits and,
- most difficult of all, the Shoulder-in and Haunches-in.

In these last two movements, the horse carries its body as though it were going to perform a Volte (eight-meter diameter circle or less) while going forwards in a straight line. In the Haunches-in, the horse crosses behind but not in front while in the Shoulder-in, the horse crosses in front but not behind.

The Airs Above the Ground require a double bridle and are usually performed by stallions; mares are rarely powerful enough. Those of the Spanish Riding School include:
- the Levade (the horse rears while carrying its hind cannon bones nearly parallel to the ground and its body at a forty-five-degree angle),
- the Mezair (a series of Levades),
- the Croupade (the horse rears, leaps up and lands on its hind legs, then puts its front feet down),
- the Courbette (a series of Croupades) and
- the Capriole (the horse rears, leaps up high enough to kick out its hind legs and lands on all fours).

In the Croupade performed by the horses at Saumur in France, the horse lowers its head and neck and gives a double-barrelled kick high enough to remove the rider of another horse.

Within the context of this book, "going forwards" includes both straight lines and movements along arcs while "diagonally forwards" is not synonymous with "diagonal line".

School figures are useful in containing overly exuberant horses by redirecting their attention as well as making any horse more supple. Illustrations and instructions on how to ride them may be found in the chapter of that name.

By "diagonally forwards" is meant a diagonal line a horse travels while carrying its body as though it were going forwards in a straight line. This is called a Half-pass and is most easily learned at a canter going in the direction of the leading leg.

Because school figures are usually done in an enclosed area, your mount is said to have an outside and an inside: The outside is closest to the fence while the inside is closest to the center.

When going sideways, a horse crosses one pair of legs in front of the other. Its legs cross in a less marked fashion when it moves diagonally forwards. No classical school work requires sideways movement. However, it is useful if you need to open gates without dismounting and is required in some western-style or police-horse work. A horse must know how to leg-yield before Turns on the Forehand or the Haunches or sideways movement can be introduced.

When turning on its forehand, a horse pivots on its inside front foot by raising and putting it down in the same place. The outside front foot moves around the inside one while the hind legs cross in their movement around the outside of the circle described in the turn.

When turning on its haunches, a horse pivots on its inside hind foot by raising and putting it down in the same place. The outside hind foot moves around the inside one while the front legs cross in their movement around the outside of the circle described in the turn.

A Turn on the Forehand is introduced via a change of direction composed of a diagonal and Half-volte on the short side of an arena. The rider asks the horse to two-track around the Half-volte portion with its forehand on an inner track.

The Language of the Aids

A Turn on the Haunches is introduced via a change of direction composed of a Half-volte and diagonal on a short side. The rider asks the horse to two-track around the Half-volte portion with its haunches on an inner track.

The school figure used to confirm a horse's mastery of either turn is called Le Carré de la Guérinière (de la Guérinière's Square). The horse is asked to pivot a quarter-turn at every corner.

From a standstill, it can go in any direction if frightened. A horse can be persuaded to go forwards, backwards, sideways and diagonally forwards provided it is set up properly.

While grazing, it can go in any direction because this gait provides an inherently stable base.

At a walk, it can go forwards, sideways, diagonally forwards or pivot on one foot.

At a trot, it can go forwards or diagonally forwards. It can also trot slowly (Cadenced Trot), even more slowly (Passage) or without moving at all (Piaffe) while displaying animation.

A horse's action is said to have animation when it lifts its feet up high. A daisy-cutter is the opposite: The horse's action is so low its toes can cut off the heads of the little daisies which grow in lawns.

Using progressively slower and slower music, you introduce a horse to the Piaffe by starting with a Cadenced Trot and going on to a Passage. Your mount must be collected and you must be adept at the gentle use of alternating Half-halts.

At a pace/amble, it can go forwards or spook. This gait's inherent instability makes it unsuitable for school figures.

The Language of the Aids

At a canter, it can go forwards or diagonally forwards (Half-pass). It can be asked to do Flying Changes, in which the horse changes leads without changing gaits. It can turn on its haunches (Pirouette).

The proper sequence of canter foot-falls must be maintained during the whole Pirouette. This is difficult enough an exercise to be considered high-school-level work.

Visually, it took millennia and a video camera to discover that cantering/gallopping horses really lead from the rear. In practice, if travelling in a counter-clockwise direction, a horse is said to be leading with the near/left/inside foreleg even though the stride really starts with the off/right/outside hind-leg.

The Natural Aids

Bar none, your **voice** is your best aid. With it, you can encourage, reward or rebuke (gently) at the same time you apply leg, hand and/or seat aids. Patting or a slap on the neck or behind the saddle is great after an exercise is successfully completed but praise is greater yet because you can give it while your horse is doing what you want it to do.

Gravity and your sense of balance hold your **weight** on your horse's back. The longer you let your legs hang down, the easier it is to keep your balance. The combination of gravity and balance gives you a **seat**. A seat like glue is necessary in performing all high-school exercises as well as extended trots and canters. You can sit them without bouncing by relaxing your back muscles into your mount's back and leaning your shoulders behind your hips.

At a walk, you allow your seat bones to move in sync with your mount's rolling movement. Actively driving with your seat bones engages its hindquarters, lowers its neck and lengthens its stride without quickening its steps. A willing horse will need no other encouragement to move.

At a canter, you also allow your seat bones to move in sync with your mount's somewhat different rolling movement. When cantering on a circle, the motion is from the inside to the outside. You use your inside seat bone to drive your horse forwards.

You halt a horse by no longer moving in sync with it, by straightening your back and driving your seat bones straight down into your mount's back. This transforms your freely moving mount into an immobile one. The more content your mount is with your presence on its back, the more likely it is that you can accomplish this without using reins.

The Language of the Aids

Your weight is hugely influenced by the direction in which you look. Horses are sensitive enough to sense the weight shift this produces even if humans are not. The more you turn your head, the more your weight shifts and the more your horse is likely to turn. Some horses are more sensitive than others but all can perceive it, even if shifting weight may not cause every horse to change direction. If your mount keeps moving in an unexpected direction, the cause may be a shift in your weight of which you are unaware. A supple and athletic rider can shift weight from seat bone to seat bone regardless of where he/she is looking.

At any gait except a gallop, you should be able to keep a sheet of paper between your seat and your horse's back without losing it. This is true even if you post a trot (also known as a rising trot).

The natural way to post a trot is on a circle. The action of the inside hind leg becomes strong enough to push you upwards and forwards off your mount's back.

You can post artificially while riding without stirrups by leaning forwards without stressing your lower back, squeezing your knees together, then rising and sitting in sync with your horse's trot. It is important to have enough of an adhesive seat at a sitting trot if you choose to try this on a horse trained to understand that "squeeze means go!"

You can also post artificially when riding with stirrups by leaning forwards without stressing your lower back, and pushing off the balls of your feet. Done correctly, your heels should drop every time you rise and return to their normal position when you sit. A sheet of paper may be kept from dropping to the ground only if you practice a lot. Done artificially, you must rise on the correct lead. If trotting a circle to the left, you rise when the outside/off/right shoulder moves forwards and sit when it moves back.

The Language of the Aids

An adhesive seat is priceless as it is your best defense from being thrown by a spooky horse.

Using **both legs at the girth** causes your mount to move forwards. The more pressure you apply, the more your horse is likely to accelerate.

This is why it is not a good idea to hang on to a horse with your legs or your heels!

A **leg at the girth** causes your mount to bend in an arc around your leg and moves its whole body sideways.

You can either leave your other leg inactive or increase the bending tendency by using both your other leg behind the girth and any rein aid which would bring your mount's forehand to the side of the leg at the girth.

The exercise I have found most clearly demonstrates the effectiveness of using just your leg at the girth is to ride a circle while posting a trot on the wrong lead. You apply pressure every time you sit. Your mount should track straight along the arc of the circle without your having to use any other aids.

Applying pressure with one **leg behind the girth** causes your mount to move its hindquarters away from your leg. This is called leg-yielding and is used in the two-track exercises which introduce high-school-level work as well as in much high-school work.

Using both your legs behind the girth will not only confuse your mount, it can cause you to tip forwards and can invite unhorsing if your mount is so minded.

The more you move your leg back, the stronger the effect unless you are riding an educated horse, in which case you need move your leg back only an inch or so to shift its hindquarters to the other side and cross its hind legs.

The Language of the Aids

Rein aids can work only if your mount is moving. Reins permit more refined movements; by this is meant more precise or minute movements by your mount. The reins' excess length customarily falls between your mount's neck and your right hand, regardless of the way you hold them.

Single reins should enter your hands outside your little fingers and exit between your index fingers and thumbs.

If you are using the four reins of a double bridle, two reins still exit between your index fingers and thumbs, and the use of your thumbs is unchanged. However, the reins associated with the curb bit enter your hand between your third and little fingers while the reins associated with the bridoon (thin jointed snaffle) enter your hands outside your little fingers. This method of holding four reins allows you to use the milder bridoon more than the harsher curb bit.

An even gentler way to hold four reins is to run the bridoon reins outside your little fingers while holding both curb reins between the third and little fingers of one hand. This means three reins exit one hand while only one exits the other. You change the hand holding the curb reins when you change direction.

If you need to hold reins in just your right hand, you place your right index finger between the left and right reins, and allow the excess to exit outside your little finger.

If you need to hold them in your left, you hold them as you would single reins, except that you place your little finger between the left and right reins.

The main disadvantage of riding with one hand is that you lose considerable mechanical action.

One part of mechanical action comes from placing your thumbs more or less firmly on the reins as they run over your index fingers. This stops them from running out of your fingers.

A second part lies in holding your wrists in such a way that a straight visual line runs from your elbow through your hand to your mount's mouth (or the end of the rein if you are using a bitless bridle). You are said to have broken wrists if you bend them inwards, outwards, up or down. This is why your nails must face each other.

The third part lies in keeping your arms parallel to your torso, with your elbows loosely close to it. This position allows you to move your hands back and forth in sync with your mount's mouth while not pulling your upper body forwards. It also gives you emergency play if your mount suddenly drops its head or snatches the reins from you.

Never pull on the reins or move your elbows behind your body. Pulling will get you a war with your mount. Needing to move your elbows behind your body means your reins are too long.

The most efficient way to vary tension on the reins is to vibrate them using your little fingers. This is why snaffle reins run outside them. Moving your little fingers does not have to affect your hold on the reins but does have a lovely relaxing effect on your mount.

The pressure on your horse's mouth should be equal to the pressure you feel on your hands. Even when you change the length of the reins, the pressure ratio should remain unchanged.

You can change their length by placing the end of the rein to be shortened under the other hand's thumb, running your hand down the liberated rein to the desired position, taking hold of it and then holding both reins correctly.

Another way is to widen the distance between your hands by loosening the pressure of your thumbs enough to allow the reins to slide, and then resume your hand position when you have found the correct length.

The distance between your hands should equal the width of your body. Otherwise you risk breaking your wrists and losing mechanical action.

Rein effects are divided into several categories: Direct reins act on the same side of a horse's body while indirect ones act on the other side. Reins of opposition prevent one leg on the other side from moving forwards. Simple rein effects are suitable for use with any horse while complex ones need considerable training.

Because the names of some of the rein effects are so long and a bit tongue-twisting, they were all assigned a number:
- the Opening Rein is Rein Effect One,
- the Bearing Rein is Rein Effect Two,
- the Direct Rein is Rein Effect Three,
- the Indirect Rein of Opposition in Front of the Withers is Rein Effect Four and
- the Indirect Rein of Opposition Behind the Withers is Rein Effect Five.

Within the context of this book, "direct" refers to the rein-effect category while "Direct" refers to the rein effect of that name.

Active and Passive Reins: The rein effect you use is called the Active Rein while the other one is called the Passive Rein. The Passive Rein's function is to assist in preventing any tendency your mount might have to avoid the effect of the Active Rein by engaging in bit evasions (See the Appendices.).

Any bit evasion means your mount is irritated with you. Some bit evasions may merely annoy you while others are downright dangerous. It is better to prevent them by improving your riding skills than by using more severe equipment. Often the opposite of the obvious is more effective than anything else. Riding on the buckle and using the weight of the reins to turn can change a horse's mind about bits.

Never use an Active Rein on both sides of your mount's mouth at the same time or you will hopelessly confuse it. Instead, alternate the Active Rein with the Passive Rein from stride to stride. Use the Passive Rein by vibrating it more gently than you vibrate the Active Rein or by just feeling your mount's mouth with your passive hand.

Using reins requires a lot of co-ordination and practice.

The weight of the reins: Some horses have a mouth so fragile they bleed if you use a bit. If a bitless bridle is unavailable, you can ride on the buckle and turn from side to side by shifting your weight and picking up the rein on the side you want to turn to with your free hand.

Such a horse cannot be trained to high-school level but it can become a marvelous trail horse provided you both learn to trust each other. It can also be a terrific school horse because controlling it effectively will force you to use your body instead of your hands. Speed is regulated by leaning forwards to go faster, backwards to slow down and by using voice commands to change gaits.

The Language of the Aids

The Opening Rein or Rein Effect One: This simple direct rein can be used in training young horses, so obvious is its effect on the untrained.

Unlike all other rein effects, you hold the Opening Rein with your nails facing the sky. The Passive Rein is held with your nails facing the side.

There should be no slack in your reins. Swivel your elbow so that your hand is held out to the side. This brings your mount's head so far to the side it must turn in order to prevent itself from falling. Vibrate both reins, keep both legs on the girth to encourage motion and look in the direction you are going. If you are actually training a horse, make sure you praise it the instant it starts to turn or you will spend a long time in training.

The Bearing Rein or Rein Effect Two: This simple indirect rein may look like a neck rein; however, a neck rein acts on a horse's neck while the Bearing Rein acts on its mouth. Your Active hand never crosses over your mount's mane. It is used primarily to produce a lateral flexion because it moves your mount's head to the side on which it is used; this motion tends to shift the horse's weight to the other side, which makes this rein effect an indirect one instead of a direct one.

In a lateral flexion, your mount bends at the poll just enough that you can see its eyeball from your position on its back. Lateral flexions are used in the Half-pass, the Shoulder-in and the Haunches-in. They are a nice touch when you bend your mount around a corner or in circling.

The Direct Rein or Rein Effect Three: This simple direct rein effect acts to slow your mount's body on the side it is used. In turning to the left, you stop allowing your Active hand to move with your horse's mouth while your Passive hand continues to be in sync. This shortens the horse's length on one side and encourages it to turn in the direction of the side it is used on.

The chief difficulty in using this rein effect lies in a human tendency to pull on reins. If your elbows can move behind your body, they are too long. Vibrating both Active and Passive Reins is key to avoiding the many bit evasions this rein effect is apt to cause (See the Appendices.).

The Direct Rein is used in the Half-halt by alternating Active and Passive Reins at each stride. Half-halts are used to slow an overly energetic horse if circling is not possible.

The Direct Rein is used to collect a horse by driving it forwards onto the bit and vibrating the reins. Eventually, your mount will yield by flexing at the poll and playing with the bit. Playing with the bit may produce foam; that foam is highly desirable, albeit messy.

Ask your mount to reverse with alternating Half-halts and driving your mount as though you were to go forwards; correctly done, it will move diagonal pairs of legs. The horse goes backwards because the pressure on its head is greater than there would be if you wanted it to go straight ahead.

The Indirect Rein of Opposition in Front of the Withers or Rein Effect Four: This anything-but-simple rein effect must be used on a collected horse. Using the off-side Rein Effect Four blocks the forward motion of the near fore while the near-side one blocks the forward motion of the off fore. Without crossing your Active hand over your mount's mane, you place your hand in such a fashion as to allow the reins to form a line from your mount's mouth to the opposite forefoot. It is used in the advanced collected form of the Turn on the Forehand. Teach your horse how to execute a simple uncollected turn before introducing it.

The Indirect Rein of Opposition Behind the Withers or Rein Effect Five: This complex rein effect blocks the forward motion of the opposite hind foot. It is the only rein effect to affect your mount's whole body.

As with Rein Effect Four, your mount must be collected. Without moving your Active hand over your mount's mane, you place your hand in such a fashion as to allow the rein to form a line from your mount's mouth to the opposite hind foot.

Rein Effect Five is used in the advanced form of the Turn on the Haunches at a walk, the Pirouette, to canter and in Half-passes. Because you use it at gaits having a rolling motion, you continue to move your Active hand in sync with your horse's motion in order to allow it to move forwards freely.

If you and your horse have advanced to the level of expertise needed to use Rein Effects Four and Five, you will know by feel whether you have used them correctly. Otherwise, you will need an experienced observer.

A Note on Artificial Aids

I have not included them in this book because, in my experience, none are really necessary in riding a horse with the possible exception of the dressage whips used to help a horse learn to move away from your leg behind the girth, or a jumping bat used in a limited and gentle fashion to persuade a mount that work is expected.

In two-track training, the rider holds a whip in each hand in order to avoid having to switch one from hand to hand. While not in use, the whips should lay across the middle of your thighs, and point backwards and outwards. Only one whip can be used at a time; it is applied by tapping your horse on the point of the hip at the same time that you use your leg on that side. The problem with using whips is that you must move your hands out of position. I have found that being patient and rewarding with my voice when I use my leg behind the girth or work from the ground is a much more positive training method.

Once in a while, a clever horse may decide to ignore its rider. My horse is just such a one. Her jumping bat is called "Conviction". I use Conviction very rarely, in the summer-time, when Tschüss is too fascinated by the clover underfoot. Usually, I just carry it. If I do use it for its normal purpose, I tap her firmly behind my leg; otherwise, I chase biting insects away.

The jumping bat is a short riding crop with a large flap at the end. That large flap presents a big bearing surface which cannot hurt a horse; it just makes a lot of noise.

Dressage whips are really too flimsy to inflict pain; they just tickle a horse's skin. They were invented to be a training device, not to make a horse go forwards.

School Figures

These diagrams are representative rather than absolute. Riding areas vary tremendously in size; you can ride these patterns in any area after adjusting dimensions.

School figures ridden on a Hunt-seat Track may be somewhat different from those ridden on a High-school Track. If there is a difference, the upper diagram on each right-hand page will be for a Hunt-seat Track while the lower will be for a High-school one.

When school figures are ridden the same way regardless of the Track, only the long sides of the riding area appear in a diagram and two different yet similar school figures will have been placed on one page.

I have deliberately avoided using the letters many riding schools use to label different points in an arena. If you have them, that is fine. Not having them should not prevent you from riding school figures.

All school figures require planning and an energetic horse. If the area you ride in contains jumping equipment, planning is especially critical.

Within the context of this book, a "Volte" is a circle with a diameter of eight meters (26.25 feet) or less. The diameter of a "Circle" is greater than half the width of a riding area.

"Across" means going across the width of a riding area while "through" means riding through its length.

Legend: I have used a thin line to mark the edges of a riding area, a thick solid line to mark Hunt-seat and High-school Tracks and a thick dotted line to mark the actual school figure. Arrowheads indicate the direction of travel.

The Language of the Aids 28

A **Hunt-seat Track** is made up of a Half-circle at each end joined by straight lines down the long sides of the riding area.

A **High-school Track** is made up of a Quarter-volte in each corner joined by two short and two long straight lines. It hugs any fence line closely, leaving you with no option but to keep your toes pointing forwards; otherwise, you risk catching them on fence posts.

Hunt-seat Track

High-school Track

The Language of the Aids

A **Diagonal** is the simplest way to change direction.

On a Hunt-seat Track, start a straight line at the end of a Half-circle and aim for the start of the diagonally opposite Half-circle at the other end.

On a High-school Track, start a straight line at the end of a Quarter-volte at one end of a long side and aim for the start of the diagonally opposite Quarter-volte at the other end.

If you are in doubt about where to start and are in a fenced-in area, start a **Diagonal** three or four fence-posts from a corner on a long side and aim for the third or fourth fence-post from the diagonally opposite corner. Count three fence-posts if eight feet apart or four if six feet apart.

If you are in an open area, use objects (cones, buckets, whatever) to mark the start, middle and end of two **Diagonals.** The only limitation is that a **Diagonal** needs to be a straight line.

If you are posting (rising to) a trot, use the diagonal line to change leads. If you are adept enough, make the change in the middle.

Change leads at a canter either with a Flying Change in the middle or by bringing your mount down to a trot at the start of the **Diagonal** and asking for the opposite lead just before you end the straight line.

The Language of the Aids

Diagonals on a Hunt-seat Track

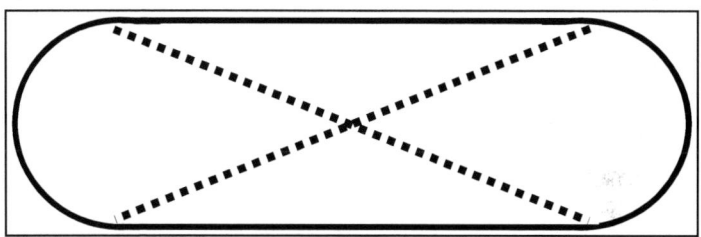

Diagonals on a High-school Track

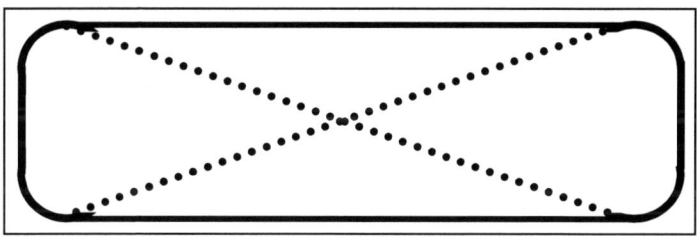

The diameter of a **Circle** is equal to, at the most, the full width of your riding area and, at the least, more than half its width. That of a **Volte** is equal to, at the most, half the width of your riding area. Its minimum size is restricted only by your mount and your skill. The larger, the greener, the older or the stiffer the horse, the less likely that it will be capable of a six- or seven- or even eight-foot diameter **Volte**.

Voltes may be done off a Center Line or a Diagonal. They may be done sequentially given a long-enough line of travel. They may alternate, with the first starting off a line going towards the left and the next going towards the right.

Horses find **Circles** hard to execute unless they are fairly supple. **Voltes** are harder yet. Always make sure your mount is able to do a big circle properly before trying them.

Humans find both difficult, usually for failure to plan and prepare. I have always found it easier to circle if I look along the arc my head will travel, on a line above the arc my mount's feet should travel, and keep my head turned exactly the same way until I am ready to end it. The more you turn your head, the tighter the arc of travel. Some horses respond more than others to the weight shift turning your head produces.

Both may be done at a walk, trot or canter. If the **Circle** is very large, and/or the horse is supple and responsive enough, circling may be done at a gallop. Circling may be the only way to bring a horse down from a gallop, provided that there is enough room and that the footing is smooth and forgiving to galloping feet.

Half-voltes are used extensively in changing direction within confined spaces, so the sooner your mount becomes supple enough to circle, the sooner they can be introduced.

Circles & Voltes on a Hunt-seat Track

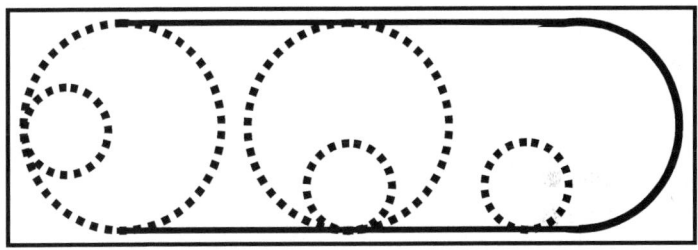

Circles & Voltes on a High-school Track

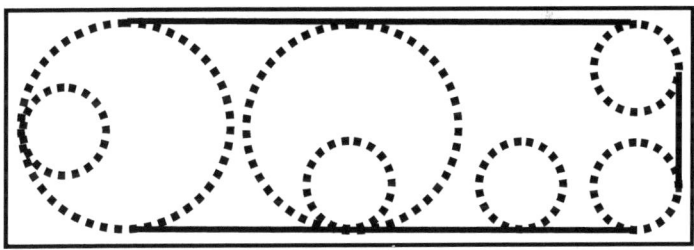

The Language of the Aids

A **Figure-of-eight** can be made of first a Circle or a Volte going in one direction immediately followed by another of the same size going in the other direction. The two must share a common point, the one at which you change leads if you are trotting or cantering.

Unless you are quite skilled and your mount is anything but green or old or hurt or of poor conformation, and unless the area you are riding in is wide enough, a **Figure-of-eight** at a gallop is likely to prove unwise.

Figures-of-eight on a Hunt-seat Track

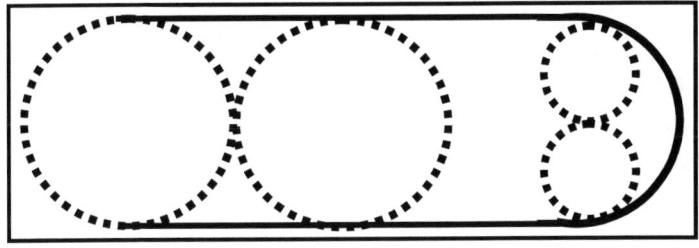

Figures-of-eight on a High-school Track

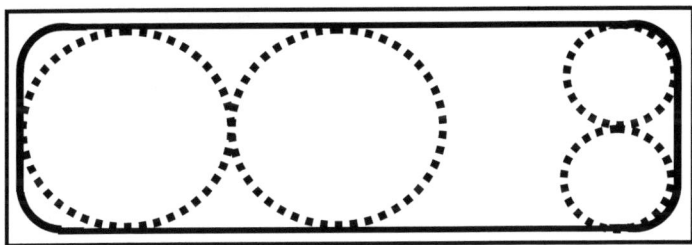

The Language of the Aids

Whether or not you change direction when going across your riding area, these school figures are performed the same way on a Hunt-seat or a High-school Track.

You can start at any point along the area's long side. The line you select to use must be perpendicular (at a 90-degree angle) to the starting track.

Whether you plan to continue in the same direction or to change it, start with a Quarter-volte. Three strides before reaching the line you have chosen to cross your riding area, bend your mount to bring it onto the chosen line.

If you do not plan to change direction, bend your mount three strides before reaching the track on the other side into a Quarter-volte going in the same direction as the first one.

If you do want to change direction, bend your mount three strides before reaching the track on the other side into a Quarter-volte going in the direction opposite to the starting one. If you are trotting or cantering, change leads on the straight line.

The Language of the Aids

No Change of Direction Across Either Track

Changing Direction Across Either Track

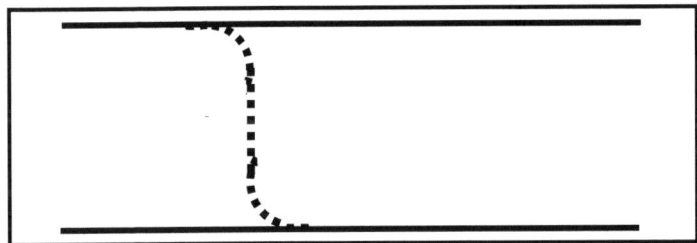

The Language of the Aids

The different shapes of Hunt-seat and High-school Tracks change the approach to the Center Line when **crossing your riding area through its length without changing direction**. Your mount must have been introduced to Voltes first.

If on a Hunt-seat Track, start a Half-volte where you normally start the Half-circle at an end of your riding area. End it at the start of the Center Line and aim for its other end. Start a second Half-volte in the same direction as your first Half-volte at a point opposite the start of a long side. Go straight when you reach it.

If on a High-school Track, turn the first Quarter-volte at one end of your riding area into a Half-volte and end it on the Center Line. Aim for its other end. Start a second Half-volte in the same direction as your first Half-volte at a point opposite the end of a Half-volte on a long side's corner. Go straight when you reach it.

The Language of the Aids

No Change Through on a Hunt-seat Track

No Change Through on a High-school Track

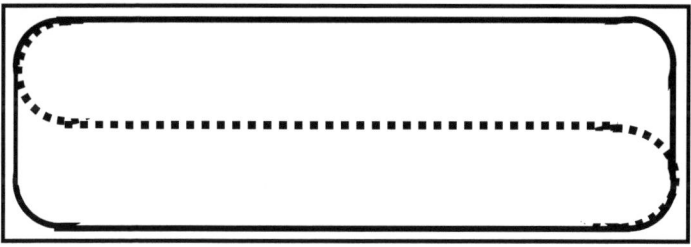

The Language of the Aids

The different shapes of Hunt-seat and High-school Tracks also change the length of the Center Line when **changing direction through** your riding area. Your mount must have been introduced to Voltes first.

If on a Hunt-seat Track, start a Half-volte where you normally start the Half-circle at an end of your riding area. End it at the start of the Center Line and aim for its other end. When you reach a point opposite the start of the long side, bend your mount into the arc of a Half-volte going in the direction opposite to your starting one. Go straight when you reach the long side.

If on a High-school Track, turn the first Quarter-volte at one end of your riding area into a Half-volte, end it on the Center Line and aim for its other end. Start a second Half-volte in the direction opposite that of your first Half-volte at a point opposite the end of a Half-volte on a long side's corner. Go straight when you reach the long side.

Changing Direction Through a Hunt-seat Track

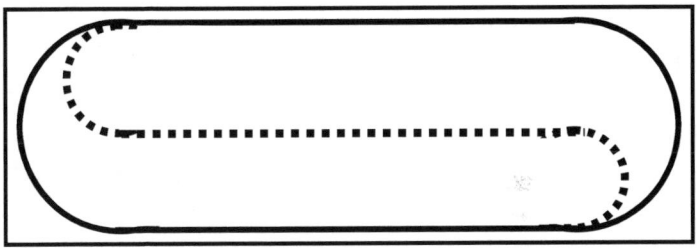

Changing Direction Through a High-school Track

The Language of the Aids

The **Half-volte and Change** allows you to change direction in a small amount of space.

Done on the long side, it can be as long as that side or as short as you need it to be.

If your mount has not yet been introduced to voltes, you can start the school figure with a Half-circle: Its diameter must be more than half the width of your riding area but less than its full width. This is true whether you are on a Hunt-seat or a High-school Track.

The end of the diagonal line should be at least a stride before the Quarter-volte or the Half-circle in the corner or end of your riding area in order that your mount has enough room to start bending in the other direction.

Most horses try to fall in, i.e., not bend their spine properly on the arc of a Volte or Circle. Many riders try to change direction by asking their mounts to turn on themselves, as it were, without asking for a proper bend.

If riding a Hunt-seat Track, start a Half-volte along the long side. It should bring you onto the Center Line, at which point you aim a diagonal line towards the side you just left.

If riding a High-school Track, you can turn the Quarter-volte in a corner of the riding area into a Half-volte. You can use the short side of your riding area as well. Otherwise, you ride a Half-volte and Change in the same way.

The Language of the Aids

Half-voltes & Changes on a Hunt-seat Track

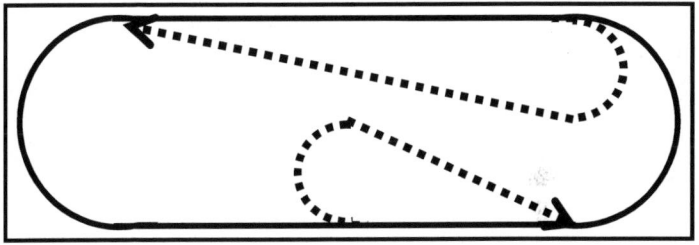

Half-voltes & Changes on a High-school Track

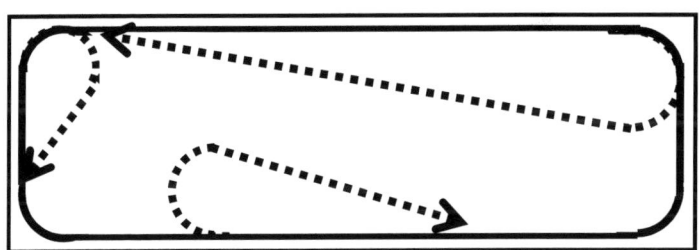

If riding a **Change and Half-volte** on a Hunt-seat Track, start a diagonal line aimed towards the Center Line once you have left the Half-circle at the end of your area. Once on the Center Line, start a Half-volte going towards the side you just left. Go straight once you get to the long side.

If riding a High-school Track, start a diagonal line aimed towards the Center Line once you have left the Quarter-volte in a corner of your area. Once on the Center Line, start a Half-volte going towards the side you just left. Go straight once you get to the long side. If your mount is supple enough, you can perform this school figure on the short sides of your riding area.

Changes and Half-voltes on a Hunt-seat Track

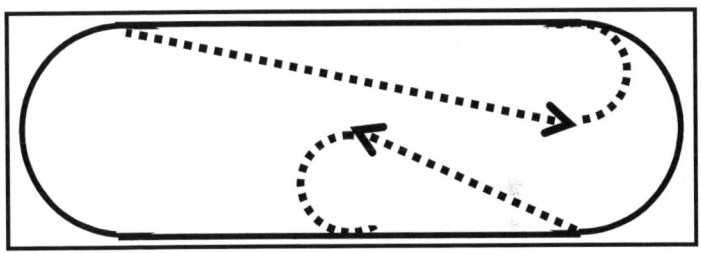

Changes and Half-voltes on a High-school Track

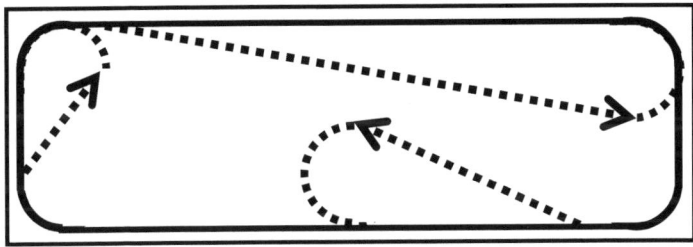

Serpentines are useful as a suppling exercise for your mount as well as an exercise for you to learn to alternate bends and straight lines. Three-loop Serpentines will not lead to a change of direction while those with four loops will. They are the same whether on a Hunt-seat or a High-school Track.

Both **Three- and Four-loop Serpentines** are illustrated on the facing page. The illustrations are for Serpentines ridden across but they may also be done through an area, providing that your mount is supple enough to bend through quite tight arcs.

Planning is vital!

Before you start a Three-loop Serpentine, mentally place straight, obstacle-free lines going across the area, a third and two-thirds of the distance from your starting end. For a Four-loop Serpentine, mentally place straight lines a quarter, half and three-quarters of the distance from your starting end.

Bring your mount onto each straight line by bending it into a Quarter-volte three strides before you reach the side. Bring it out of each straight line with a Quarter-volte three strides before you reach the opposite side. Depending on the length of your riding area, you may or may not have enough room to have a short straight line on a long side at the end of the exercise.

Go straight at the end of a Serpentine.

Three-loop Serpentine on Either Track

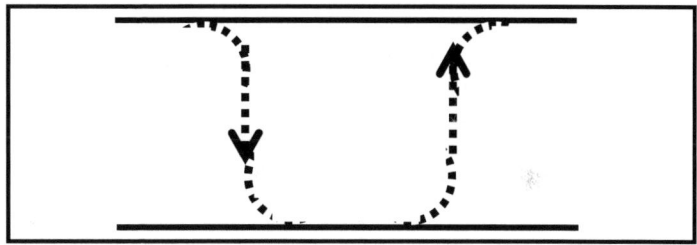

Four-loop Serpentine on Either Track

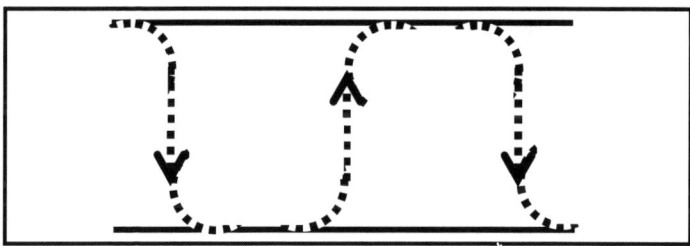

If riding in a circular area, it is even more important to change direction frequently than in a square or rectangular one because it is harder on horses to bend constantly than it is to travel on straight lines with occasional bends.

Plan before you start. Mentally split your circle in half. Bend your mount into a smaller arc which will bring it onto a straight line, then bend it again to reach the outer track going in the opposite direction.

If you are riding in a small area, it is suggested that changes of direction be done at a walk.

Changing Direction Within a Circle

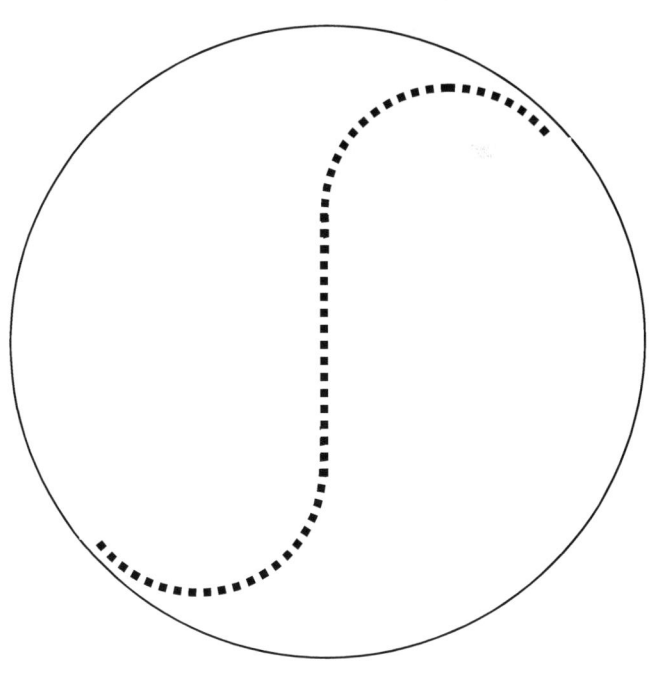

The **Flying Changes Serpentine** may be done without Flying Changes at a walk, or with them and with Half-passes. It functions to supple your mount or distract it from the distracting while it can help you learn to ride short and alternating diagonal lines.

The angle of any Apex (point at which you change direction) should be no tighter than 90 degrees.

You can ask your mount to keep its body facing the line of travel or you can Half-pass (your horse's body is held parallel to the school figure's edges while its body goes along a diagonal line). It must cross both in front and behind to accomplish this, so an observer might prove useful until you learn how it feels when done correctly.

This school figure can be done out in an open field or on a bridle path provided it is wide enough.

Flying Changes Serpentine in a Hunt-seat Arena

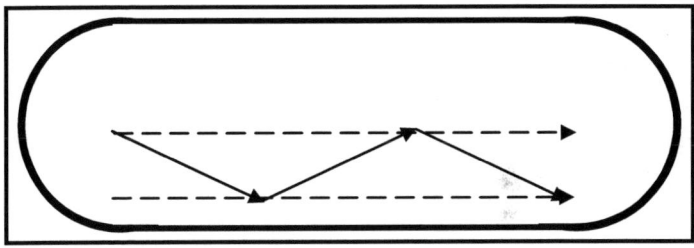

Flying Changes Serpentine in a High-school Arena

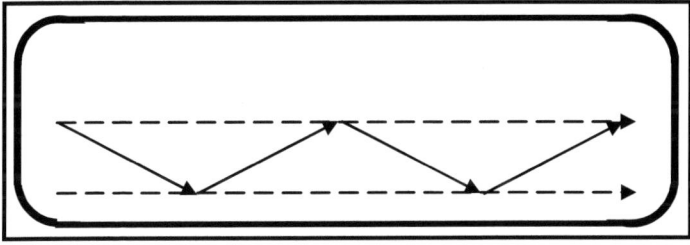

Use the **Carré de la Guérinière (de la Guérinière's Square)** in a walled area to train a horse to turn either on its forehand or on its haunches. The walls prevent your mount from moving forwards when it should be pivotting. The first side should measure the same number of strides as the other three and always goes towards a wall.

In Turns on the Forehand, the distance between a corner and a wall should be equal to the distance between your mount's forefeet and its nose when held in its natural position plus about six inches. In Turns on the Haunches, the distance between a corner and a wall should be equal to the length of your mount's body from its front feet to its tail plus about six inches.

In performing a Quarter-turn on the Forehand at each corner, use the side of the Square to energize your mount, check its forward speed with a Half-halt when its forefeet are where the pivot should take place, and turn its hindquarters towards the outside of the school figure. Once its body is parallel to the wall, stop using your turning aids and ask your mount for a straight line parallel to the wall.

In performing a Quarter-turn on the Haunches at each corner, use the side of the Square to energize your mount, check its forward speed with a Half-halt when its hind feet are where the pivot should take place, and bring its forehand onto the next straight line, parallel to the wall.

Once you have done the Carré/Square two or three times, change direction.

Your mount is ready to move on to half-turns or full turns when it can pivot properly at each corner, whether on its forehand or on its haunches.

An observer can tell you whether pivots are being performed correctly.

The Language of the Aids

Carré de la Guérinière for Turns on the Forehand

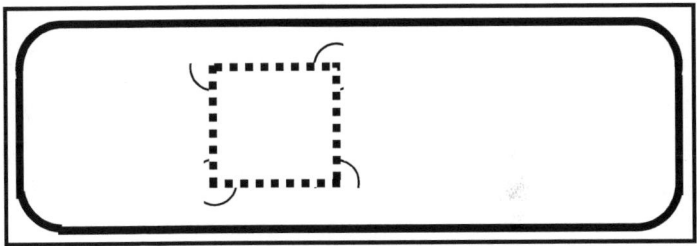

Carré de la Guérinière for Turns on the Haunches

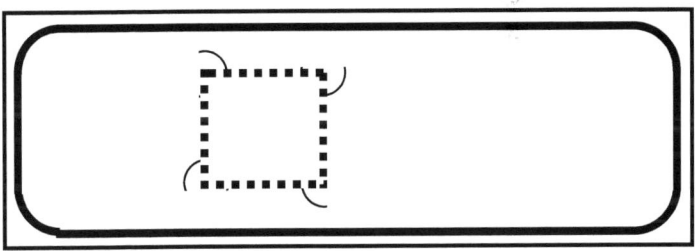

I invented this **Cloverleaf** to help quell my sometimes overenergetic Tschüss when only wide open spaces were available to ride in.

It consists of alternating voltes and short straight lines. The sequence of the arcs does not really matter. What does matter is that your mount pay attention to you, not to that horrifying whatever-it-is out there. You can use Circles instead of Voltes if you have enough room and your mount is not yet supple enough to be doing Voltes. That said, Voltes are more suitable than Circles because their smaller size makes them physically more difficult and captures the attention of fractious horses faster. Excess energy is more readily bled off with Voltes.

In the past, when I used to trail-ride in Europe, I had similar problems on bridle-paths. I found that alternating **Loops & Lines** had a positive effect on getting control of horses wanting to go to Timbuktu at the speed of light.

The Language of the Aids

Tschüss's Cloverleaf

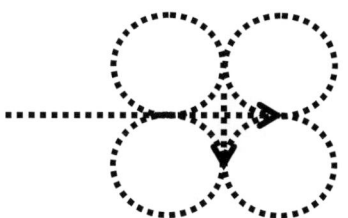

Loops & Lines

The **Spiral** is very useful in introducing a horse to progressively smaller arcs of travel; it is best done while rising to/posting a trot.

Bring your mount onto the largest possible Circle in an area free of all obstacles. Slowly and surely, ask for more and more bend. Only a very supple horse can make the smallest Voltes and great care must be taken to make sure your mount does not lose its balance. For the most part, keep the diameter of any Volte to at least one-third the width of your riding area. Reverse the direction of the Spiral once you have done one or two of the small-size Voltes and progressively go out to a full-size Circle. Follow with a **Spiral** in the other direction.

Drills

A **Drill** is a series of school figures ridden with two or more horses. There may be two people or forty, although, if forty are riding together, all should be capable of controlling their mounts under any circumstances. Drills require the ability to control your mount's speed relative to the speed and position of other horses both in the now and in the future.

One of the simplest consists of two Files (think Indian File), each using a separate Diagonal to change direction. Imagine that you are in a group of eight. Start by counting yourselves off from one to eight. You split up by riding through the area. Odd-numbered riders turn left at the end of the Center Line while even-numbered ones turn right.

Whenever riders travelling in opposite directions need to be in the same space, those in the File of Odd Numbers stay on a track close to the edge while those of the File of Even Numbers ride a track in the other direction at least six feet away from the riders on the outer track. The six feet constitute a safety zone, lest a horse or horses not be keen on being close to another going in the opposite direction.

If riders are inexperienced in keeping pace with other horses, Diagonals shorter than the norm may be used so that there is more space at the ends of the riding area for the two Files to cross.

At the start of the first possible Diagonal, the first rider in each File turns onto the Diagonal at the same time. The following riders should keep a three-horse distance at this point. At X, where the two Diagonals and the two Files meet, each even-numbered rider cuts through behind each odd-numbered rider. Use the distance between X and the end of each Diagonal to close up the distance between horses in each File.

At the other end of the Diagonals, the riders in the File of Odd Numbers stay on an outside track while those in the File of Even Numbers stay on an inside one. Make sure to stay six feet apart and ride as close to nose-to-tail as is safe so that the lead horse on the inside track does not risk running into the last horses of the opposite Diagonal as they come to the end of their line of travel.

When going down the long sides, the first odd-numbered rider can be ahead of the first even-numbered rider and a distance of three horse-lengths should be maintained in both Files.

At the end opposite to the one where the Diagonals ended, each rider should merge into a single File going down the Center Line. Odd-numbered riders precede even-numbered ones.

Everyone turns off in the same direction to end the Drill.

Or imagine that you are in a group of five. Counting off is not necessary for this Drill. When all are on one of the riding area's long sides, everyone turns across and changes direction on the other side. This can actually be done safely when little distance separates each horse provided that the skill of each rider is equal to that of all the others at being in control. This is because everyone must turn onto a line across at the same time, walk/trot/canter across while lined up on the first horse, and turn onto the opposite long side at the same time.

The possibilities are almost endless and are limited only by the abilities of horses and riders, the size of the space you ride in, the weather and the footing.

Conclusion

Once you have mastered how to use the first three rein effects singly, you can start combining them with the other natural aids to see how they can work. Knowing how a horse is physically able to move at any given gait is essential in choosing which aid or combination of aids to use.

Your voice, seat and leg aids as well as Rein Effects One and Three can be used with all the work all riding horses should be able to do in order to be riding horses, regardless of your style of riding. You can also ride bareback with a halter or bitless bridle.

Rein Effect Two requires a bitted bridle.

Rein Effects Four and Five, used in conjunction with many other aids or, in the case of number Five, alone, are used only on trained high-school horses and also require a bitted bridle.

High-school work can be done while riding bareback provided your seat is adhesive enough; however, you will need a snaffle bridle. Your seat should be as glue if you ride bareback with a double bridle since you need particularly quiet and gentle hands to use it.

Enjoy!

Appendices

63   *Bit Evasions*
65   *Rider Removal*
69   *Just Having Fun!*

Bit Evasions

A horse can try to evade the bit by:
- *grabbing the bit between its teeth.* Counter by riding on the buckle.
- *snatching the bit which whips the reins out of your hands.* Counter by riding on the buckle.
- *sliding the bit out of its mouth.* Counter by reducing pressure on the side the bit slid to, increasing pressure on the side it slid from, vibrating both reins and driving your mount forwards.
- *raising its nose above its ears.* Counter by lowering your hands and vigorously driving your mount forwards.
- *glueing its nose to its chest.* Counter by riding on the buckle.
- *shaking its head.* Counter by reducing pressure on your mount's mouth and driving it forwards, or by riding on the buckle.
- *wiggling the length of its spine, also known as having a rubber spine.* Counter by using natural aids to straighten your mount and driving it forwards. Rubber-spined horses are unsuitable for all but experts since a lot of co-ordination is needed to ride them.
- *popping a shoulder (the horse seems to lead with it).* Counter by using a Direct Rein and a leg on the girth on the side of the popped shoulder, your other leg behind the girth and driving your mount forwards while looking where you want to go, not where your mount wants to go.
- *bolting (the horse runs away at top speed).* Counter by bringing your horse down to a walk and walking it until it is cool and dry. A horse may also bolt out of fear, in which case you should re-assure it constantly as well as cool it off.

Rider Removal

For the most part, Rider Removal happens because a horse has been unsuccessful at getting its message across about being unhappy. They may not be a personal attack on you but are rather a result of an accumulation of previous unhappinesses. Some can be ridden safely bareback with a halter, under which circumstances you the rider have less absolute control and the horse has more say.

The better you treat the horse(s) you ride, the less it/they will be interested in practicing Rider Removal!

All but one manœuver have been performed on me. I am glad that that one has not come my way because I do not see how a rider could walk away afterwards.

Rearing straight up can be countered if your reflexes are quick enough. Before it can get completely upright, you must lean forward, grab the mane close to the ears, dig your heels into its sides and, if you have a crop or a jumping bat, hit it hard behind your leg. Otherwise, you will need to jump off and get away from the zone where the horse might land on you if it topples over. If you are successful in your counter, remember to let go of the mane, take your heels out of your mount's sides and return your body to an upright position as the horse returns its own body to a more normal position. Get it moving forwards as soon as its forefeet touch the ground: Moving horses cannot rear.

Rolling may also be countered if you are quick enough. Your mount must put its head down to be able to lie down. Pull its head up and apply your heels with vigor: Moving horses cannot roll. Otherwise, jump off and get out of the rolling zone. I can personally attest to the discomfort produced by being rolled on.

Scraping may be countered only if you are aware that your mount practices this technique of using something solid and immovable to get rid of you. The horse swerves so close to a tree or a post that there is not enough room for your knee in the saddle! The counter consists of using a bat hard on the side of the swerve or by swinging your leg onto the horse's rump for just enough time to get past the immovable object. Which you use usually depends on whether there is a branch low enough to wipe you off the horse's back! I was lucky: The horse chose a cast-iron support pillar in an arena, I was warned that the horse "had its tricks" and I could see the move coming. The horse only tried once.

Bucking ranges from flinging out hind feet while moving to breath-robbing leaps into the sky. I have been exposed to three forms, the flinging out of hind feet at a canter, crow-hopping (the horse hops up and down four feet at a time like a pronking antelope) and sun-fishing (the horse twists in the air while airborne). Staying on is a matter of skill and/or luck.

Spinning uses centrifugal force to fling you to the outside. If you are successful in countering it, it will be because you are quick enough to lean to the inside of the spin.

The **Removal-by-dropped-shoulder Manœuver** consists of waiting until the rider is leaning forward and slightly to the side. The horse drops the appropriate shoulder and the rider falls off. It may not always be possible to avoid. A horse I knew in England used to stand still while getting rid of its rider in series of three or five. It would drop its left shoulder to pull the rider's body into position. I was exposed to the first of a series of three; since I was too old to risk my bones to the potential of more, a younger rider got the second and the third.

The **Tennis-ball Manoeuver** consists of using the saddle as a human uses a tennis raquet to hit the human's posterior like a tennis ball. A horse does this by dropping its hindquarters suddenly and then bouncing back. There is no counter because there is no warning! It is 100% effective.

The **I'll-go-one-way-while-you-go-another-way Manoeuver** is equally effective: While you are still leaning forward after going over an obstacle, your mount suddenly jinks to one side. You continue going straight ahead! I hit my helmetted head on a steel post holding up the arena's roof and saw my instructor in triplicate.

The **Gallop, Stop-in-my-tracks & Drop-my-head Manœuver** works on all riders, regardless of skill. I somersaulted three times before landing on my hunt cap's button. The young horse I was having a jumping lesson on had decided that lunch was more important than learning. Its jumping lesson was extended another half an hour and it never repeated that Manœuver.

The last one applies physics most efficiently. I saw it on a TV clip of a rodeo. Instead of bucking, it reared straight up and stuck its nose up above its ears. Once the rider was basically dangling at the end of the reins, the horse stopped rearing and snapped the reins by putting its nose on its chest. The rider's body described a perfect arc over the horse's front end and hit the ground. He did let go of the reins before he touched down. The horse, with the bucking strap still tight around its tender zone, just trotted off.

This well-thought-out Manœuver took less than 8 seconds. Ouch!!!

Just Having Fun!

Some horses play under saddle. Tschüss is one of these: She carefully waits until I am not paying attention to her, then leaps up in the air and takes off at a gallop.

My reaction the first time she did this turned out to be the correct one: I laughed and she stopped gallopping.

"*Gotcha!!*"

Had I punished her for it, I would probably have turned her into a horse keen on rider removal.

About the Author

Christine Wolfe was fortunate to have learned from French cavalry officers who had served in the North African non-mechanized cavalry. Her instructors were not world-famous but their riding heritage was solidly grounded by their need to be good horsemen in order to stay alive. She also had instructors who studied at the Ecole Militaire de Paris, an equestrian school created in 1751 by Louis XV.

Her gods of equitation include François Robichon de la Guérinière (1688-1751), father of classical French equitation; Colonel Alois Podhajski (1898-1973), former director of the Spanish Riding School in Vienna; Janou Lefèbvre-Tissot (1945-), who represented France in the 1964, 1968 and 1972 Olympics; and ex-jockey André Sagaud, now-unknown trainer of Nelson Pessoa of Brazil.

Since 1991, she has owned Tschüss, an energetic purebred Trakehner mare around whom life revolves.